TURNING SIXTY

TURNING SIXTY

POEMS BY GARY MIRANDA

𝒵

ZOLAND BOOKS

Cambridge, Massachusetts

First edition published in 2001 by
Zoland Books, Inc.
384 Huron Avenue
Cambridge, Massachusetts 02138

FIRST EDITION

Library of Congress Cataloging-in-Publication Data

Miranda, Gary.
Turning sixty : poems / by Gary Miranda.
p. cm.
ISBN 1-58195-034-9
I. Title.

PS3563.I69 T87 2001
811'.54—dc21

00-067308

Book design by Janis Owens
Printed in the United States of America

05 04 03 02 01   8 7 6 5 4 3 2 1

For Dominic and Virginia Miranda,
who gave me, among other things, life.

Acknowledgments

Some of these poems have previously appeared in various magazines, as follows:

American Scholar: "For John Crowe Ransom"
Aspect: "Premonition"
Audience: "Cockroach," "The Bus," "After the Storm"
Colorado Quarterly: "Phaleron Beach"
Confrontation: "Love Letter #2"
Descant: "Rope Trick," "Vigilante," "Ghost Writer"
Image: "Eve in Eden," "God's Grace," "The Role of the Arts in Education"
London Magazine: "Yannis Ritsos on the Island of Samos"
Malahat Review: "Sonnet for Salvadore"
Minnesota Review: "The Pig"
Motive: "The Revision"
Northwest Review: "One-Night Stand"
Omphalos: "Distances"
Poetry Northwest: "Item," "Poem for the Body"
Shenandoah: "Day of Departure"
Story: "The Monster of Bad Orb," "Milk Creek," "Definition"
Tar River Poetry: "The Retreat," "For A Boy on the Bench"
The Colorado Quarterly: "Milk Creek"
The Far Point: "The Exam Committee"
TransAtlantic Review: "Mice"
TransPacific: "Directions into the Poems"
Yankee: "The Fox," "To St. Christopher," "To Isabel," "Something Important"

A special thanks to Gina Phillips for her kind permission to use her watercolor painting "Tricycle" on the cover of this book.

Author's Note

Both the title and the timing of this collection may be misleading. A critic, coming upon this book, might reasonably assume that these poems represent "the poet's mature period," whatever that might mean. Similarly, readers familiar with my earlier books might assume that this third collection contains work done over the fifteen years since my last book of poems appeared. Neither assumption would be correct. Many of these poems were written before *Listeners at the Breathing Place* (1978), and all of them pre-date *Grace Period* (1983). Having noted as much, I should probably explain.

I stopped writing poems in 1982, two years after I became a father. I had discovered, by that time, that I could not support the dual passions of poetry and fatherhood, and it seemed clear to me which would have to go. Partly because of my background as a Jesuit seminarian, I suppose, I viewed poetry as a vocation, a sacred calling, and I wasn't interested in writing poems as a hobby. My decision to quit did not feel like a sacrifice, though I was surprised at the time that it didn't. The long and short of it was that the Muse simply couldn't compete with my two-year-old son. It wasn't even a contest.

My son, Nicolas, turned eighteen in June of the same year that I would later turn sixty. Shortly after he departed for a year of travel before beginning college, I found myself rummaging through old boxes, looking for — well, who knows what I was looking for? What I found was some twenty-years-worth of poems that, for one reason or another, had never made it into book form, though many of them had been published in magazines. I'm not sure when the idea of collecting some of them into the present volume occurred to me, but I completed the task on my sixtieth birthday.

This book, then, is a kind of birthday gift to myself. Compiling — and in some cases revising — these sixty poems has given me much joy, and I pass them on out of my long-standing conviction that it is in the nature of a gift to be shared.

G. M.

Contents

The Celery Prince

Of Foreign Lands and People

Boston and Beyond

THE CELERY PRINCE

Directions into the Poems

Go to the door marked "Enter."
Do not enter. Talk
to no one. Wait. In two
minutes or so some lines

will appear. Follow the lines
around the back and into
an alley. As soon as you enter
the alley, echoes will talk

to you in double-talk.
Do not listen. Enter
a window, ducking the clotheslines
first. Once you are in, two

critics will come in too
and arrange themselves in lines,
one-deep. Ignore their talk.
Leave by the door marked "Enter."

(Do not enter into
talk about these lines.)

Sonnet for Salvadore

Of Salvadore the Celery King I sing.
Illiterate in Lewiston, he'd wander,
so I'm told, into the ladies' john
and, barring ladies, not suspect a thing.
But when it came to celery, he was king.
And when he died, the *Idaho Daily Sun*
said: Salvadore the Celery King Moves On.
The celery hung its head, remembering.

Sometimes I think I'll wind down Lewiston Hill
(where winding up and winding down's the same
except for purpose), enter past the mill
and, turning to face the crowd, announce my name:
"Gary, son of Dom the son of Salvadore
the King, whose throne I've come to claim."

Wisdom

For William Stafford (1914-1993)

As though God were a bear,
lumbering in a kind of half-sleep, thunder-
stepping this way and that, all
sense of direction purely a matter
of instinct, making up
what he doesn't know as he goes along,
until, haunch-deep in our lives, he calls
them "winter," and settles in,
"Wisdom," you say, "is having things
right in your life."

And as flakes accumulate
like words when we know we're wrong,
like a bad case of the blues,
only white, and all over the forest
earth is climbing trees almost,
or else the trees are sinking,
bare limbs clawing for help
while the true bear sleeps, its own claws
tucked under, soft as snow, but warmer,
you add: "And knowing why."

God's Grace

Sister Petra, second grade,
said: "You should make it clear
to the class that the lion
in your attic isn't real."

A sacrament, she'd told us,
was a visible sign
of God's grace. "My lion
is a sacrament," I said.

Later in the day, the sky
began to fall, white flakes
resisting at a rate
that didn't matter enough.

I raised my hand and asked:
"If gravity's real, why
do the trees grow up? Why
don't they start in the sky

and fall?" When she
took away our lions,
she gave us saints.
It was something.

Eve in Eden

Blame ripened like strange fruit in his eyes —
how could she avoid them? And she was aware,
lately, of other signs: the tiger's sheer
agility conjured danger; dark skies
strained toward even darker meanings; when flies
stitched their hieroglyphics on the air,
her fingers twitched, impatient. Everywhere
she looked, warnings broke like bird cries.

And she who had named the weasel, ibis, snake,
who had conjectured "rain," watching it fit,
would find herself at night lying awake
beneath the anonymous stars; or she would sit
for hours watching him sleep, confused by the ache
of dailiness, and knowing no name for it.

Vigilante

He manufactures foes as rabbits
rabbits,
and declares:
"It's rabbit-hunting season."

He needs no reason
for splitting hares;
because they're *there*
is good enough.

And should you ask, "But *are* they?"
he would scoff
and turn you out of doors,
or in.

And should you say,
"But the rabbits above were
only metaphors,"
he'd grin

and have *your*
number, RABBIT-LOVER.

Mice

For Robert Peters

You felt like a peon, you said.
Like a child, you meant. Like
Richard, your lost son, or
yourself, shadowed into a minor
death in a wood in Wisconsin.
Because

later you mentioned mice. One
had blundered into your office,
droop-whiskered, underfed, paws
like tendrils, all-but-dead from
hunger.

"Not even the books have glue
these days," is what you said.
Sad is what you meant. *Dead*
is what you meant. *Mouse, our-
selves, our children, wives — oh
everything is dying!* is what
you meant.

I have learned what *your*
mice mean.

The Pig

For Theodore Roethke (1908-1963)

*"Pigs, like poets, are never appreciated
until dead."* — PROVERB

On the tennis court
the pig is clumsy: catches the ball
on his grovelly snout.
Oink! says the pig. Furi-
ous, a real fart-snorter,
he rushes the net
in a portly flurry
of hooves and haunches. All
the bystanders gather
and stare: you'd just as soon
not let it be known
you're there together.

But O in his pen
how he dances, dances:
a diddle-y pig, a fine
pig; turns and twirls at his nicely
best, a tender
pig. He would chuck you under the chin
then off, pirouette precisely
off, leap-pig over the fences O
and down the road, O
down the road:
a pig you would have been proud
to know.

The Fox

For DeWayne Rail

"I always wanted to be a fox," you said.
Singularly unequipped for foxhood,
you scribbled poems about some scavenger lad

who'd scurry down sewers the cops could never find
him in, living on pilfered apple rinds,
grapes (in season), and the gleanings of his mind.

I mention it merely, as one who knows hawks
from handsaws, hide from seek, and who likes
in you what never would have made it as a fox.

Child

What are you, my tipsy riddle,
in your yellow slicker and knee-high boots?
— to yourself, I mean.

Your arms ta-*tum*
to the skip of your feet
and your hair keeps time like a softy snare.

A parade, perhaps?
A maker of rain?
A one-child shivaree?

You cannot stop to answer.
I hadn't meant that you should.

The Basic Two-handed Shift

The trick is that the right hand acts as a cov-
er mainly, and shouldn't move at all. The other —
the left hand — does the work. First, leave

a standard little-finger-break above
the card you'll want on top (you needn't bother
noting it). Improvise some live-

ly patter if you like, then slowly shove
the little finger of the left hand further
in and side-slip the upper portion of

the deck, allowing the lower half to piv-
ot upward. Clear the corner, bring together
the halves (reversed now), thus completing the move.

Be careful lest the edges "talk" and give
you away. The sound should be as soft as a feather
brushing against the fingers of a glove.

Ghost Shack

The grass slants to the right
like exclamation points
in italics. One wonders
what it could possibly be

excited about. The shack slants
too, and the crates around it.
Even the trees. This scene
is going nowhere fast

and won't take *yes* for an answer.
The screen door, torn,
flaps in the breeze, a crude
attempt at communication.

Off to the side, one twisted
tree looks over its left
shoulder, stumbling, hell-bent
for the nearest town, to warn them.

Great Aunt Becky

She seemed to get old
in italic bold,
like a *personage*.
If the world's a stage,
she exited right.
Rising, she cried,
"I'm having another
attack — don't bother
to call the nurse!"
I prepared for the worst
(I was probably eight),
my eyes footlights
to her final scene.
"What do you mean
another," grandmother
said. "The others
were all pretend!"
"This is the end!"
Aunt Becky vouched
as she fell on the couch
in a heap, and died.
None of us cried,
nor did she expect
it, I think — though I suspect
she found it odd
that we didn't applaud.

For A Boy on the Bench

It's no disgrace. Still, if there were
cheerleaders here, you know their eyes
would flash "nice guy," that kinder version
of "finishes last." If in the stands
your father (but there are no stands,
and your father, who mostly went to your
brother's games, is dead) were watching,
he would fashion elaborate stories for
his lawyer buddy's sake about your old
injury, the coach's grudge against you,
how once you scored a final basket to win
the game, the series, the All-State
title, his buddy all the while squirming
on his fat-pad of credit cards, and knowing.

And you know too, though what you know
grows parent-like in its caring forget-
fulness: the fishing trips you never got
to go on, the kittens you couldn't keep,
that baseball glove you got one Christmas
that didn't fit your little league of notions:
embarrassed, you managed to parse
one complex sentence of gratitude, then
went out in the convenient world and lost it —
just as your team is losing now while you
sit on the bench, helpless, and that platitude
"It isn't whether. . . , son, it's how. . ."
falls short of the basket, and the scoreboard
clock runs out like your father's credit.

For John Crowe Ransom
In His Eightieth Year

Let the dead bury the dead —
seems a likely price to pay.
April down your days instead.

Bones that yours have comforted
lightlier lean to black decay;
let the dead bury the dead.

Go is green and stop is red;
April is green and means to stay.
April down your days instead.

Thomas the Stern and Tender Ted
finished their work and went their way —
let the dead bury the dead.

Hardy's in the garden bed
getting colder day by day;
April down your days instead.

All I have to say is said;
nothing now remains to say.
Let the dead bury the dead;
April down your days instead.

Retreat

I can't remember whether it was the cows
or the wild rosebushes that came off
as better companions, but somehow
both seemed interested in what I said
as I hacked at the stubborn roots. I suppose
the cows — I wasn't killing *them*. Really,
I wasn't that keen on killing the rose-
bushes either, or anything but time —
thirty days of it, no talking allowed.

To people, that is — my fellow Jesuits.
This happened in Oregon, some century
ago, the hills there as green as I was.
All that rain. I remember standing
in rain one day saying the Angelus
only to look up and find the local
bull two feet from my dripping face.
A papal bull — infallible, huge. I learned
the meaning of retreat that day, all right.

But the rosebush business — that wasn't just
sport: they would have crowded out the grass
for cows. I thought of them as the last
vestiges of vices I was out to lick: anger,
disobedience, lust. I kept a long list
tucked inside my cassock. Take impatience:
I worked for hours on that before busting
my pickax on a buried stump and throwing
the goddamn handle at a passing cow. Just

now what stumps me is why I should happen
to think of this — like suddenly noticing how,
all morning, you've hummed a particular tune.
I haven't seen a cow in years except
on a billboard or a Ben and Jerry's van.
I probably wouldn't know a rosebush if
I sat on one, and the thing I'm sitting on
is a Greyhound bus, writing this, trying
to work up my nerve to talk to that woman.

Definition

She moves too close, almost, for poetry.

> And has the added dis-
> advantage of being
> slightly incredible —
>
> except to butterflies
> and fellow creatures that
> grow from the inside out.

> Effortless,

she weaves herself around her as she goes.

> For sake of counterpoint,
> plays Ariel to my
> Caliban, Virgo to
>
> my Sagittarius.
> As lexicon, supplies
> the synonym for "love":

> She is mine.

She is one by whom others are defined.

Ghost Writer

For John Dempsey, S. J.

Last night word came in a dream
    that you were not really dead,
        and I believed it.

You came to me then to confirm the news,
    your face puffy and yellow
        as if diseased.

I'd pictured you teaching the dead diction,
    telling them: *Nouns and verbs*
        are always better

than adjectives, and: *Never use*
    the passive voice, or a sentence
        that starts "There is. . ."

Ghost, I heed the notes you've left
    penned in your cramped hand
        and pinned to mine.

The Revision

Marching through the snow with never a green pine in sight.*

*Ed. note: This line was later revised by the author to read:
Marching through the snow added to the urgency of the situation.

— FROM *POEMS OF MAO TSE-TUNG*

You change the line as if
there being no green pine in sight
had something to *do* with the urgency
of the situation. And you may be right.

In Seattle I wax pacifist for the clan,
"Coo coo" my way through living rooms until
I grow to be a joke, even in my own eyes.

But down around Laguna they look sideways
when I pass, and tell me that my
pipe, and naked face, and yellow golf hat
(not for golf, but for my growing thin on top)
leave little room for hope.

I used to think: there's a spot in Oregon
where, driving through, I'd cancel myself out
like an equation. Or, better still,
where I could stop and climb a hill and,
under a green pine, pull myself around me
like a shirt and *be* what I am.

But that was before I started turning thirty.

Now I am less concerned with why no green pine
grows in sight, and more with how this
marching through the snow adds
to the urgency of the situation.

The Exam Committee

"Re-read Shelley — it can't kill you,"
they tell me, as I decompose,
unnoticed, before their eyes.
They talk of integrity — the department's,
the exam's — everyone's but mine.

They begin to debate among themselves
what "Prometheus Unbound" is all about,
and while they are thus preoccupied
I slip out and down the hall,
convinced there's a better way to die.

And I see myself as sly John Clare,
loose from the loonhouse,
hoofing it north on the Great York Road
past Jack's Hill, Baldock, Biggleswade,
and Bugden, out of Essex.

OF FOREIGN LANDS
AND PEOPLE

The Monster of Bad Orb

It was when my feet began to freeze that I began to seek the
enemy. I knew they would probably shoot me, but it
didn't matter. I fancied the flow of blood from the
wound as warm and rich. I would watch it as it oozed,
red on the white snow, until I died, and I would forget
about my feet.

But I would not lie down now and go to sleep in the snow. Until
my brain froze I would not lie down like some animal, like
woodchucks I used to find in the woods in Illinois, their
luminescent entrails ravaged by birds and maggots —
pointless in the pointless woods. I would find the enemy,
the Germans, and let them shoot me because it mattered,
because I was important.

To keep my mind off my feet as I walked, I thought of those at
Bad Orb who had *not* escaped — Sperry, Steingass, Buck —
and wondered if they were thinking of me. They pictured
me, no doubt, in Switzerland, in some ski chalet, with an
Alpine maid in a peasant blouse fixing me warm wine.
Buck would say, "That bastard!" and throw down whatever
he had in his hand. The rest would think their own thoughts,
plan their own plans, and wait. I envied them their patience. I
envied them their false visions of me.

I looked down at my feet. The pieces of gray blanket I had
carefully wrapped and bound were stiff and anonymous,
like packages that have been mailed and remailed until the
lettering has worn away. I had to concentrate to remember
they were mine. I watched them. I heard their steady *hinch
hinch* in the snow — as if they knew where they were
going. But I could not feel them. I began to think of them as
companions, wiser than I was, guides that I must follow. It
would be foolish to get separated now. I could never find
my way alone.

I reached the edge of the sparse cluster of gray, leafless trees I
had been wandering through and found myself on a hill
overlooking a small village. I had no idea where I was. This
could be Switzerland, but I doubted it. Bad Orb, we had
been told, was in the middle of Germany; Switzerland far to
the south.

As I started down the slope I noticed that the dried stalks poking
through the snow were all pointing in the other direction —
back up the hill — and that the needlepoints of the wind
were coming toward me, into my face. I told myself it was
an omen. But my feet — battered, determined — were
unconvinced. And I followed them.

I began to suspend my mind. It was a trick I had learned in the
camp — to let the mind float the way the body can in
dreams when you jump and decide to stay there in the air.
It never lasted, of course, but I had practiced until I could go
for an hour at a time — longer if nothing interrupted me.
We started down the hill together: my feet, detached but
physical in the snow; my mind floating above. The rest of
my body was nowhere — the invisible string between kite
and boy on a windy day in October — nowhere.

I don't know how long I walked or when I became aware of the
voices, and then of the shouts. I don't recall seeing any
faces, or even any houses. But the shouts were clear, and the
tone was one I knew — fear, almost panic.

I expanded in my mind to an invading army at first, and then
merged into a figure I had seen in an old movie:
Frankenstein's monster, blundering — slow, huge, awkward
— into a Bavarian village. I remembered my feet — I did not
see them — and they matched the image so well that I
actually raised my arms full-length in front of me and curled
the fingers into tense claws. All around me was turmoil and
confusion: the sound of feet running on boards; shouts in
some throaty, hysterical language. Clearly, I *was* important.

I could have stepped on their houses, their children, and crushed them without an effort. I knew, from the movie, that guns would begin firing soon, and that I must die slowly and with dignity, and that they would realize — later only, and with remorse — that I hadn't intended to harm them.

The crack I finally heard didn't sound like a gun at all, but more like a damp twig breaking. I felt no pain, only an abrupt sensation of heat in my right shoulder, and I took it as a signal. I went down on my knees in the snow, paused, and then, arms still stretched out, forward onto my face.

The rest is not important — the other camp and what came after. This itself would not be important except that still, at casual gatherings and without warning, when the talk of those around me begins to grow at times senseless and remote, I feel myself inside me begin to turn back again, and I hear in my mind the monster of Bad Orb coming — the steady crunch of those awful feet in the snow — and see that blue-gray face, those eyelids frozen shut, those raw, stiff hands extended, and I grasp the sides of my chair, hard, until he passes.

To Isabel
Who Hid in My Closet in Buenos Aires

I found you there, knees tucked up
like the elf they hang on Christmas trees,
in your pink orphan's uniform and your brown
eyes. I found you there on Christmas day

trapped between my trousers and my shoes.
Trapped between ages: old enough to try
and try well; too young to see the folly
of the plan. As if I *could* take you with me;

as if when the ship sailed you would be safe,
forever; as if my home were anywhere
that Argentina wasn't, a place that walled no
children in, a fortress against time.

You spoke in Spanish, sobbing, and I did not
understand — which is to say, I did, but turned you in
anyway: to the other world, the real one, to adults
who run the orphanage, the proper authorities.

You return, Isabel: on off days; in the faces
of children in Valparaiso; in the black mirror
on the back of my closet door where I crouch
in a darkness of my own. Waiting.

In the Netherlands

Outside my door the Dutch maid
rattles her keys. She'd have me leave,
so anxious she is to begin the sad
ritual of the dust rag. If I gave

her twenty guilders for her care
and asked her to go away, she'd shake
her head instead and "Nee" like a mare.
She knows, as I do, what's at stake:

the encomiums she pays to brooms
reinforce the ancient curse.
Shake your locks and keys till dooms-
day, Beelzebaby. Do your worst.

Vienna Foursome

For Al Salsich

We started out in the Griechen Beisl that winter
night, where a man, whose face couldn't believe
his fingers, played the zither. The snow drove
by like a taxi shifting gears in inter-
mittent traffic. We made ourselves the center
of that cold world, we four, content to live
and let live, more than happy to be alive,
then braved the weather to Stephanskellar and dinner.

Such things add up. A life grows if you let it.
Who's to say where nights like these might go,
given a taste for laughter? Like a doughnut
you dunked my wife — or she, you — in the snow.
And if I loved your wife a little — and who wouldn't? —
does it matter? Can you tell me? Do you know?

The Fierce Dogs
(August 25, 1900[1])

Once you had fierce dogs in your cellar:
but they have been changed at last
into birds and sweet singers.
— FRIEDRICH NIETZSCHE

One, gnashing its teeth down on the small
bones of a dead rat, drove me insane
with the sound. Every night after that

I would hear it and wake in sweat
screaming the names of my children, except
I had no children. Another's trick

was licking the sores on the private parts
of prostitutes, a feat which earned it
the name *Moonaki* — Greek for *vagina,*

which is Latin for "cunt." Still a third
developed a snarl so fierce — and hackles
the size of houses — that, lying in bed

in the twilight of idols, I would light
my fingers instead of candles as a
burnt offering to the gods. And there

were others, too gruesome to mention.
But they, like these, have been changed
at last into birds and sweet singers.

Listen!

[1] *Nietzsche, insane, died on this date at his home in Naumburg.*

31

Milk Creek

When I fired,
the sniper fell
from tree to water not
as if he had been shot
but more like some awkward
boy daring his first dive
and bringing it off —
but not quite,
not with style.

And sequence switched to a stream back
home we used to call "Milk Creek"
(distance tells me now what
nearness missed — that it was "Mill" and
not
"Milk" Creek — but never mind),
where, if you tossed a chunk of crawdad in,
the fish converged from everywhere
and battered so thin
so fast the thing they fought for
that it disappeared
like magic; and where the wind
skimmed down the channel like a bird,
ruffling the shallow
water with its wings, and turned
the corner with the precision of a swallow.

We used to dive there
and knew the depth and where
you had to turn up quick
so not to scrape the rocks.
And it was easy — once
you learned the trick.
But courage faltered
the first time and I stood for fifteen
minutes on a stump,

confirmed in my reluctance,
till Pat Sharp laughed
and called me chicken,
and I jumped.

It jolted back and struck then
sudden — *Christ,*
he didn't come up! He must
have hit a rock, been
hurt; he might be down
there bleeding now and someone ought
to save him! Dave Bowdoin
clapped me on the shoulder with "Good shot."
And I remembered:
I had killed him with intent,
and this was not
Milk Creek and had never been,
though now and then
a wind skimmed along the river like a bird,
ruffling the yellow water as it went.

Acknowledgment

SAD NEWS NAOMI KELLEHER PASSED AWAY
AFTER BIRTH OF SECOND CHILD
FUNERAL 11-13 PLEASE ACKNOWLEDGE

I played tonight the guitar you gave me,
 cracked now beyond trueness,
  beyond help.

Across the long indifferent Atlantic
 they are letting you down gently
  into the earth,

while here on my cluttered desk the telegram
 sits like a dumb receipt for something
  I didn't buy.

Why don't you ever write? you said
 in the edges of your last letter.
  I didn't answer.

But I played tonight the guitar you gave me,
 trying to raise on my soft fingers
  old calluses.

Remembering Your Names

For my students at the University of Athens, 1970-1973

You were easier to teach than stones,
but only slightly, and your names
were longer than a long rain
when children have to play
indoors and are not happy.
Whatever I had to say

to you I tried to say
like Demosthenes with stones
in his mouth, making happy
noises to the sea. But your names
tripped me up like a play-
on-words in Greek or rain-

slick marble steps. "But rain
is beautiful," you say;
"As children we used to play
in Plaka though the stones
there were slick as glass. Our names
are all like that — happy."

OK, forgive the unhappy
metaphor; forget the rain.
I was talking about your names
and how I could not say
them. Your names were sharp stones
stuck in my shoe, a play

of five acts within a play
of five acts that has no happy
ending: the hero stones
his unfaithful wife in the rain-
soaked streets of, say,
Seattle, calling her names

I will not repeat, names
no sane man can afford to play
around with. "But listen," you say
again, wanting me to be happy,
" — they are as beautiful as rain,"
skipping the syllables like stones.

And today, while the play of rain
on stones is trying to say
your names, I listen, happy.

Yannis Ritsos on the Island of Samos[1]

If you kill me, I will give up, but if I live,
I can stand worse than this and still sing.
— ASKLOPIADES OF SAMOS

His wife gone to the mainland to find
what medicines she can,
the poet adjusts his lamp,
his life.

"To go to Samos," the Turks have a saying,
"is to go to one's death." But a Turkish proverb cannot
be trusted. Medicines cannot be trusted.
Still. . . .

From the pocket of his thin jacket he removes
the thin pad of a waiter — his foolscap.
It pleases him, this quirk from his prison days;
the pad fits his hand like the hand of a friend.

But the hand of a friend. . .the kiss. . . ?
The gestures of fear mimic the gestures of friendship,
closely. He has learned this: a knock on the door;
a hand on the shoulder; words:

"You have only to write for permission
to leave, to go to Athens. You are, after all, a free
man. You are, after all,
a Greek."

Pain he can trust. It begins to stumble again in his groin
like a blind man using a sword for a cane, or a scream
heard through a door that opens and shuts, opens
and shuts.

On Samos, Ritsos, bent, eyes clenched into fists,
presses his forehead against an open waiter's pad
and waits: for a woman. . .belladonna. . .
atropine.

[1]In 1967, though suffering from tuberculosis, Ritsos was sent by the Greek
junta to the once-German prison camp on Yura in the Aegean. In response
to international pressure, he was later removed to the island of Samos, off
the coast of Turkey.

Greek Girl with Child

She thinks of little else
these days. When friends come
they wonder why she needs
cheering up *this* time.

A boy from Salonica
has offered to marry her,
not knowing how it is.
She does not love him.

She thinks, as she dresses,
that things never work out
the way you plan — a not
new thought, but she is young.

Her uncle — her doctor —
told her that there was no chance
of mistake and that she must
make her decision soon.

Her little brother, two,
watches from his crib,
jabbers, wants to play.
She fastens her bra

and tries to decide whether
to wear her panty hose
under her corduroy jeans.
Her mother says if she doesn't

she'll get blisters on her heels.
One uncle, her mother says, died
from blisters on his heels.
She skips the panty hose.

Downstairs the family waits —
not for decisions, but breakfast.

They are fat with ignorance,
she thinks. She lifts the baby

from the crib and starts down.
The baby talks, but she
says nothing. She cannot know
how her voice will sound today.

Cockroach
(Phaleron, Greece)

In the kitchen, as I open the refrigerator,
a cockroach.

There is no verb to equal his movement
to under the rubber lining of the door.
He was here. He is there.

I get my can of bug spray from under the sink.
I spray the rubber lining.

The cockroach falls, landing upright,
on the ledge of the door above where the eggs are kept.

I spray him again.
He does not understand it.
His fine antennae grope like a mind waking to bright light
in a strange place.

His tan-enameled body folds like a sneeze, and unfolds;
folds like a sneeze again.
He goes on his back and his feet thrash
like a secretary's fingers:
he types his final testament on the air.

I imagine the fist-grip of his stomach
as his movements become slow,
as his feelers extend straight out on either side.

I advise him to die, but he does not heed:
his white underside and the down of his legs still thrash.

There's no future in it, bug.

I curse the spray that does its job so slowly.
I curse my own squeamish refusal to squash him
once and for all.

And I think, *Did the neat names on the marble slabs*
in the Phaleron War Memorial
die like this?

And I think — I think of Andromache
weeping for Hector
dragged over rough ground like a plow,
face down.

Greek Bus

What must a man do to deserve his death?
Not any death,
but *his*.

For the death of the thin-faced man who drives the bus
day after day
from Phaleron to Athens
is different, surely, from any other —
different even from the death of the man
who takes the tickets:
a talkative man, heavy-set,
who pats the heads of children as he passes
or, if he stays in his minute booth in the back,
hums snatches of Greek melodies, out of tune.

What must they do, these two, to deserve their deaths,
their separate deaths?

Or on the side-seat — there, facing the sea —
the lone man
fingering his beads,
marking the bright waves with his dark fingers!

Love Poem with Bats

Say my love for you is the particular
application of a general rule, the rondeau's
refrain hammering back on itself, or
the irrelevant difference between stalactites
and stalagmites as viewed by insomniac
bats. Solids outbalance stripes and prints
in the wardrobe of absolute color.

On such a night as this, Rimbaud
fastened his foolscap to a lamppost
with a bandanna and wandered out
of poetry with his life, if not his mind,
intact. Coleridge lay weeping at
the insoluble hunger. Hitler sighed,
longing, perhaps, for a simple daughter.

My love for you is as simple as that,
as complicated as that, like
Rappaccini's daughter tripping on
the philosopher's stone, or Madame Bovary
transplanted to Odessa as the alto
soprano in an all boys' choir. We must alter
our expectations, not our standards.

Phaleron Beach

We combed the beach one August dawn,
our camp clothes damp from sleeping under sky.
I walked and watched the dirty sea
belch undigested kelp along the curb;
you lingered slow behind, looking
in your ghostly sun-bleached hair
a little like Cochise grown old,
yet childly serious.

Your hunt was not for buffalo but feathers,
stones, the skeletons of fish:
you cradled them into your fate-found paper bag
like wounded birds.
Those too large you called me back
to share your wonder with,
then made me executioner
to save you the pain of discard.

I cannot fathom your feel for lifeless things,
cannot approve removal from their age-intended place,
but feel for you as you must feel for stones,
would polish and preserve you
as you were there, then — Ann,
you gather in my mind like pools the tide leaves,
here and there a freckled stone
flashing into remembrance.

After the Storm

Scattered pieces of broken boxes, a doll's
head, the leg of a table, a lensless pair
of glasses, a valise, the tattered blue
fin of a diver, a child's sandal, innumerable
jags of marble, slate, debris.

Strangest of all, a shell — so seldom
seen here — with the living thing inside still
living, beginning to peek out
into the rubble around a fringe
of polished orange — alert, ready.

I lift it; touch the flat, brown flap. The life
retreats, slowly, like the pulsing of a wound,
or the fall of an eyelid when a word
has pierced its blue film and touched
the whiter, inner eye.

I replace the shell and move on down
the beach. The flat-stacked jut of stones
I had made my own is gone, leveled
to the shoreline, but scrambled now
beyond design, beyond intention.

Nothing remains as it was. The beach
is another being entirely. Incredibly different.
A stranger. And the sea — mindless, irritating —
sucks on the stones, retreating, like a child
playing with a straw when the juice is gone.

I climb the bank and wait for a space in the traffic.
Along the divider someone has stacked,
in evenly spaced piles, cut grass to be hauled away.
We shape our lives out of what we find.
I find a space. . .I take it.

Although You Say No Future

My love for you
has roots like wild
rosebushes
that scatter across the whole hillside of me.

We could talk to a cow about it,
a ruminating one
who would take his time
and offer no easy answers.

Or:

I could take this page
and shape it into a flower
whose petals would leap out at you
at the slightest touching,

giving you
at least
the rough
idea.

Day of Departure

All day we go around not speaking
except when necessary.
Words, as a rule, turn sour
in the Greek sun
or are burned down to chinky cinders
that would confuse even the cleaning lady.

You give instructions on what to send,
what not to send.
I listen. I look out windows a lot.
The birds on the opposite roof today
are a muted chorus,
their fidgety bodies firm in one direction.

In the vacant lot behind our apartment
two cats are making a big thing out of bushes,
have some cause in common that is urgent with noise
until, fed up with nature,
the grey-and-white one walks away,
indifferent as water.

There are parades planned,
streets marked off in white lines for the band,
as if it mattered.
The sea itself is a surface sheen,
nothing more. The day
is calm as a calm mistake,

and the only threat of alarm
is the one I hold inside me,
careful as broken glass:
the pieces of our years together that,
dropped now, would make an obscene sound,
like: *Stay!*

One-Night Stand

We staged our last farewell
on a well-kempt lawn with footlights.
Overhead, a neon horseman whirled his
come-on. The parking lot was packed, but
restless: headlights wandered in and out,
in and out, anxious for action.

And when you cried, who were so unused
to cry for me, cues crumbled and lines
dispersed like a nest of serpents startled.
And I, past care of headlights, held you,
friended and fathered you at once — oh
clothed you with myself, no casual lover.

Out front the motors coughed, embarrassed;
this was not what they had come to see.
Moving patterns on the backdrop told me
they were leaving — us, with our rehearsals
shot to hell and clinging to no hope of
good reviews but only rocking, rocking.

Our love scenes lunge away from strangers.

The Cleaning Lady

In the dustbin of the soul there are no places
that escape her, no cobwebs of intricate surprise.
Her eyes have eyes. Like her transistor radio,
she has her frequencies, and knows her station.

She tunes in an appropriate soap opera —
a plethora of platitudes, all true —
and during the commercials talks of you:
When is Madame returning? is the question

she never asks and, never asking, answers.
Obstinate as stains on underpants,
she soaks my life's clothes in her solution:
one part Joy, ten parts perseverance.

If I disconnect the phone, if I move away,
she'll reach me through the long phone of the grass.
She has informers. They telegraph through trees,
or pass the word from mouth to mouth of leaves.

Until she goes, I squirm at her unmercy.
Afterwards I go from room to room
and every one enunciates that same
scrubbed-bright syllable: your name.

Distances

In this country outside Salonika,
in any countryside,
things happen in distances —
dogbarks, basketball bounces, mountains:
in the distance, Olympus, snow- and cloud-capped,
mimics any mountain — a cliché.

In the distance too, birds make sounds
I expect live birds to make. But coming closer,
I notice that they run down, like Christmas toys
that operate on batteries. Approaching now a row
of cypresses, I hear the noises birds perform in secret
in these times, their small motors fluttering.

Overhead, a magpie (orange and purple and
taken by mistake in black-and-white) doesn't understand,
and says so. I don't understand myself — *either,* that is —
bird, but never mind. If the crones of the cypress stay
till spring we will begin again, you and I,
and baffle *them.*

Meantime, it is winter, it is Christmas,
it is Greece.
And all these birds are leaning toward Byzantium
in their thick shades, toward
some first, some simpler meaning,
toward — *say it, my sparrow soul!* — home.

BOSTON AND BEYOND

To St. Christopher

(On hearing of his removal
from the Canon of the Saints)

If it wasn't you, who was it then
who got me safely this far?

And what did you and Barbara
and Boniface of Tarsus *do*
to get yourselves scratched from the list?

Chris, you disappoint me.
I expect to hear, tomorrow,
that Shakespeare really *was* Marlowe;

that Apollo XI never left Cape Kennedy;
that Jesse James is alive, and living
in Amity, Oklahoma;

that all those born the year I was
are being recalled for defective parts —
the heart, probably.

Where do I go from here, Chris?
And why in hell am I asking *you?*

Planes

Outside the window of this plane, not even
clouds. Just white space modulated by
white configurations, little intaglios
of sky portending — what? The mind, thrown
back on its own resources, opts for optimism.

Up here the air's so thin that the voice
of whatever god you live by rations words
like water. The pilot tells you things like,
"Half the flying time between Chicago and
Seattle is over the state of Montana,"

and you listen, wishing those little white
things were sheep in a snow storm in Billings
and the stewardess, soon, would announce:
"We're going out to play now; the backs
of your seats will serve as sleds." Strange,

then, how planes, seen from the ground, seem so
peripheral, like words in a dictionary that we
refer to only when someone says, "Look up. . . ."
Sometimes the sky lets go of one, but even then
it lands in the headlines next to our grapefruit,

where we pass it casually, moving on to the comics.
That people *live* in them seems as remote as intelligent
life in City Hall, or the unlikely shape
of our own lungs. And yet there are loved ones
up there — *here* — no more insured against breakage

than you are, lunching at Schrafts's or lugging
your clothes to the laundromat. Caught in such
a predicament, let us connect — long distance,
collect, whatever — because there are no phones,
and lightning is a sad wireless to remind us.

Undercurrents

1.
All day the wind blew.
Spray flew from the backs of waves
like horse's manes, white or gray.
On the beach we huddled together
until the needlepoints of sand
drove us back over the dunes to woods
for a little shelter: trees just starting to
think "Leaves" in the face of the wind's
"Forget it!"

2.
By evening the wind
had changed its mind. Fishermen sat,
each with his own lantern, and watched
or didn't watch the taut lines vanish
into the black. "How can the sea," you said,
"since it's coming towards us, pull the lines
tight like that?" "Undercurrents,"
I said, and you believed me.

3.
Later still, at the only pub in Newburyport,
we sat and listened to folk songs, sat
through three performances until
the tired proprietor flashed the lights
and we walked back to our small room
with the yellow curtains.

4.
The next day we read in *The Boston Globe*
that a sixteen-year-old boy
had climbed a telephone pole in Newburyport
and been electrocuted, and that all the lights
in all the houses in town had dimmed
for a brief moment.

Love Letter #2

First of all, forget my previous letter —
the one on guilt and innocence in Milton.
Insert, for the above, a sprig of olive,
which blooms, in season, right outside my window.

Wait. Insert instead the tree it came from —
a primary source, shades of Return to Nature,
shades of a tree (I think I'm on to something).
A tree — that's it! No, wait — make it two trees,

three or four trees — five — a half a dozen,
a sea of silver-green on black, and moving!
I come! I come! Wait for me in the arbor.
If I'm not there by sundown, start without me.

Memory

Her name
keeps slipping my mind
into something more comfortable.

Busses

I rode a bus today — from Somerville
to Harvard Square — hardly far enough
to find a seat, or need one. Still,

finding one, I thought of you, who rode
for more years than I've lived
busses to and busses home from work;

of how we'd come to meet you, down
55th, past Albright's Grocery, Pit-'n'- Pat's,
and you, crossing the street, would watch

for traffic, pretending you could die, then
shade your eyes against the sun to catch
a glimpse of sons on bikes, and smile.

When the world demanded exact
change, you said: *What's wrong with tokens?*
Dad, you're right, and this is mine.

I could have walked today, or taken the car,
but even for this short distance, I'm
with you: on a bus you can relax; on a bus

you don't have to watch the road;
on a bus you can let the reassuring engine whir
like love, knowing your stop is coming,

but not yet.

On Finding Rail's Photo
in *Down at the Santa Fe Depot: Twenty Fresno Poets*

"Squirrels could never resist one look at me."
— DeWAYNE RAIL

The beard you have in the picture
is the kind of beard you *would* have:
it shuns your face like the eyes of a nun
hearing a dirty joke. I like it.

Remember the joke about the bald Armenian
midget? A pool shark, I think. *Was* he
Armenian? A midget? I know he was bald,
balls in all of his pockets. Well,

your hands are in yours. And your jacket
looks like a piece of posthumous prose
composed by a posthumous prose writer.
Your eyes are anthologies I'd read, but

I would widen your smile, tack one end
in Gertie, Oklahoma, the other in Fresno.
You could ride it, boy, like a sway-back bronco,
amazing your friends, making your family

forget your failures at farming. As it is,
I'm tacking your photo to trees in Harvard Yard.
Squirrels are ecstatic, chattering, "Shoot
me, shoot me!" Do you make appointments?

"Relax," I tell them. "Rail is stalking
the universe — sort of. When last seen,
he was down at the Santa Fe depot, headed
this way, picking off squirrels like proverbial

ducks in a barrel, or poets in Fresno."

The Friend

I had a friend
who killed himself.
Simple as that.
He slit his wrists
with a razor
blade and lay face
down on a bench
and died. They found
him there last week
in the locker
room where, he told
me once, he used
to long to smooth
his palms along
the thighs of young
boys entrusted
to his care, and
sometimes did. I
can't remember
what I said to
him that day or
whether my eyes
slid away from
his; but reading
the news of his
death today from
one who tells it
like the weather,
I begin to
ransack my desk
for paper clips,
oblivious
of what it is
I hope to hold
together. "Shit!"
I complain. "Why
can you never
find anything
when you need it!"

Something Important

On my lap a cat named
Buick purrs, idling,
as I idly stroke her
haunches. A beautiful thing,

I note, though I don't like
cats. I've never met
a cat who didn't know
something important

I didn't know and
wasn't about to tell me.
And there's that famed
curiosity, not idle

like ours (the need, say,
to see who's next in line
in the therapist's
waiting room) but rather

the absurd assumption
that the world has nothing
better to do than hide
cat surprises

in out-of-the-way places.
"Cats are trees with their
headlights on," I tell her,
just so she'll know I know.

She stirs, curious,
then settles in again.
Some beautiful things
never learn their name.

The Role of the Arts in Education

For Alan Myers

Jacob, after wrestling an angel all night,
awoke the following morning with a great
feeling of exhilaration and a slight

limp. Whoever wrote that story never said
how this affected his later life — whether he had
a hard time getting the girls or, like Lord

Byron, overcompensated for the limp
by becoming a roué, or if the handicap
put him in poor stead for whatever he happened

to do for a living. My own guess — as good
as the next person's — is that he probably led
a pretty normal life — marital strife, bills, bad

dreams — except that his neighbors, unimpressed,
had to remind him, "Look, the center of the universe
you're not, Jake" — which, of course, he was,

as were his neighbors, who, industrious and down-
to-earth, spent their whole lives without even
seeing an angel, let alone wrestling one.

Eye Witnesses

One tall boy, a long way
down that aisle, stands
like a dying plant rooted
in rock. Even his hands
do not know what he wants,
and are tired of guessing.

At twelve he's already been
busted for drugs, in jail
and out again, his parents
shrunken under the massive
door and he, like a Martian,
moving, unfriendly, toward them.

The blue eyes of squad cars
define the octagonal shape
of his dreams, their light
converging over his head to
dead center, like streamers,
his mother shouting "Surprise!"

And there are those other eyes
that stare from the brazen
T-shirts of girls at school,
telling him — what? What
message of his might cause them
to harden, and stay that way?

"If you *mean* breasts, then
you should *say* breasts," his
teacher admonishes him today
in the margin, as if she
could know what he means. But
she is the teacher, has breasts,

and her words stick like burrs
to the nap of his thought, that

sweater he is always almost
wearing. One day, he thinks,
he will learn how not to pick
at his chin, how to imitate

men who ask questions and wait,
their eyes like stilettos,
for answers: the salesman who smiles,
"How soon were you
expecting your guests?"; the ex-
marine who knows guns.

Tonight he will grind his teeth
into her imaginary bones
as blue lights flash in his
father's eyes, which close,
concealing the word for breasts
that might have named *his* softness.

Item

The paper said:
    In a Minnesota prison
    an Indian named Dean White
    hung himself last night
    for no apparent reason.

The report read:
    Dead: White, Dean
    (Indian). Weapon: Curtain
    sash. Motive: Uncertain.
    Age: About thirteen.

If You Are Discontent

Go out into the darkened streets
and follow the sound of any siren
till you come to a place where a Black boy
lies on the sidewalk, covered by someone else's
coat and a young White nurse in her whiter
uniform bends to attend him.

From where you stand in the small
cluster of onlookers, gaze into the boy's
eyes, that are alive and moving, and notice how
they hold you off, how they hold off, even,
all these faces that bob above him, as a juggler's
hands never seem to let the falling objects land.

Then, if you can, imagine beneath the impersonal
coat a bullet hole — a red center — and, again
if you can, enter the small mouth of that cave
and crawl in and in till all light fails and even
the distant sirens hum no louder
than the blood in the veins around you.

Here you must listen carefully for the sound
of breathing, but not your own, and follow that sound
till you come to a place where a knife of light
slashes the black like a minor sunset. Seeing that slit,
you must curl yourself into a tight ball and think
yourself large again, little by little, holding back

at first but then bursting forth from the boy's mouth
as a long scream. As soon as you have done this,
resume your former shape and try to appear
inconspicuous: buy an evening paper, lose yourself
in the crowd, walk home. . . . This exercise,
if done properly, need never be repeated.

Value Is Relative

A cat is to a dog
as poetry to prose,
as woman is to man,
or eyes are to a nose.

Value is relative
in these things as in those,
but think of Oedipus
putting out his nose

instead of his eyes, or his cat.
Doggies, think on that.

The House that Derek Made

had scribbles where the attic should
have been. You could say that. Kristin,
who was also five, told him he was

crazy, and she meant it. Her
house had windows where the windows
should have been, a house you'd call

a house, unqualified. Derek drew
a square that was a door, then cut three
sides so that the door would open. Once

inside, he knew enough to know
that furniture is only one dimension
of the real, and not the most engaging

as houses go. His attic stairway
bridged the gap between what's seen
and known, as one might greet a living tree

as what it is, a friendly sibling —
except that Derek's attic wasn't
friendly. "That's not the way

to draw a house," Kristin insisted, flatly.
"It's not any house you know," he answered.
He might have said: "Failure to believe

in ghosts is one of the ways we under-
estimate God's sense of humor," but he
didn't. Against the grain of Kristin's

solid house he went on drawing attic,
stairway, scribbles — "house." He called it
what he called it. But he knew.

Womb

Goethe, leaving that place, exclaimed:
"More fluid!" I like to think so.

Traveling from there to here our bodies
back up, like those wheels in movies

that spin in reverse as the stagecoach
plunges forward. What do we think

we could *do* back there? Leave a note?
Instructions on how to love us better?

And yet it isn't "back" exactly. Whatever
it was that wanted out, still wants out.

Premonition

Nothing forgets like the sky.
My breathing has never believed
in courage. If I should die,
what I have done becomes my life.

The area all around my heart
has voices like you get on the line
long-distance that you know do not
belong to the living person

you called. Inside my bedroom
wall is the nest of a small mouse —
maybe. I lie awake, a broom
next to my bed — just in case.

Slot Machine

She owns the machine.
Or it owns her.
You cannot be sure at first.

She straddles the stool in her chocolate dress,
her ass hung over the edge —
a fudgsicle starting to slip on its stick.

The machine is making promises to her —
ching and *ching* —
lovin' her up with its one good arm.

She leaves it only to get more change,
glancing all ways first,
snuffing the handle with a paper cup — her mark.

Hours later and the last trip made
she turns the dirty cup face down.
The sag of her jaw defines "incredulous."

She cannot believe the machine's last words.
An orange, it says. *Two oranges,* it says.
A prune.

The Volunteer

*"What we need is a volunteer police force
to rid our parks of muggers, queers, and
other undesirables."*
— A LETTER TO THE EDITOR

He wears his uniform with pride.
The sun's his symbol, stitched in red,
with yellow rays, upon his sleeve.
When he arrives, the pigeons leave.

He likes his limits well-defined.
And though his closed, uncluttered mind
has forfeited all notions of
brotherly, or other, love —

no matter. He performs his part
with ardor that would warm the heart
of Herod, and his skills preclude
regret, illusion, gratitude.

Poem for the Body

You move in your own direction,
away from wherever it is
the rest of me would go.
You have a previous engagement.

The things you do amaze me,
and the things you don't.
And so I follow behind unbid,
subservient as a dog.

Attentive, I attend your school.
We major in Temporary Significance.
We will wear diplomas for clothes
and graduate with honors.

Only in mirrors you escape me,
or in the rooms of dark windows
where you pass — alone, inanimate.
In case of fear, I will break the glass.